THIS BOOK IS Cute!

SARAH WASSNER FLYNN

NATIONAL GEOGRAPHIC
KiDS

WASHINGTON, D.C.

Contents

Picture this ...

A tiny, fuzzy puppy looks up at you with big eyes. It has floppy, velvet-soft ears and it's wagging its tail. It's small. It's vulnerable. You can't help but want to cuddle it. Puppies are just so cute!

But what exactly makes adorable things so, well, *aww*-some? It turns out there's a biological reason you melt into a puddle when you see a puppy ... or a baby ... or that sweet teddy bear you squeeze at night. Studies show that we are naturally drawn to cute things because they actually trigger powerful emotions within us, making them more appealing. This is the science of cute.

And it doesn't just impact the way we interact with babies, puppies, and kittens. The science of cute also has a lot to do with how we go about our daily lives, from the toys we choose to play with to the clothes we buy, the places we visit, or what we want to eat. Cuteness even has a big impact on business! People have dedicated entire careers to adorable items. And believe it or not, cuteness also plays a major role in our culture.

So, from the cuddliest creatures to the cutest mini meals, the squishiest robots to darling fashion designs, this book will explore all things adorable. Flip the pages for fascinating facts, plus photos that'll make you squeal with delight—all while discovering the science behind why there's so much more to sigh-worthy things than just being, well, cute.

CHAPTER 1

OH, BABY!

LET'S START AT the very beginning. Literally. You were born to be cute. All babies are! (Even your annoying siblings!) And researchers say that how we interpret cuteness in other things is based on what we love about babies. In fact, back in 1942, a German researcher named Konrad Lorenz dedicated an entire study to it. He came up with the term *kinderschema* (German for "child form"), which says that baby beings—both humans and animals—all have distinct characteristics that combine to up their appeal. Read on to find out what exactly makes babies so darn cute—and what's going on in our brain that triggers these make-you-melt feelings.

Born With IT

THERE'S JUST SOMETHING ABOUT a baby that's undeniably cute. Make that some*things*. As theorized by Konrad Lorenz, infants have many distinct characteristics that, when combined, produce one perfectly adorable package.

Seeing CUTE

People have different preferences on everything from their favorite foods to their favorite colors. But when it comes to what we consider cute, all humans are basically born with the same ability to recognize—and prefer—adorable things. According to a 2014 study, kids as young as three prefer pictures of puppies and people with "cute" features, like big eyes and a rounder face, over images of adults. In the study, experts tracked the children's eye movements and noticed that they spent much more time looking at the classically cute images than at the others. Here's looking at you, cute!

LOWER EYES AND EARS

A baby's eyes and ears rest lower on her face because her skull is still forming. They'll move up as her cheek and jaw bones develop.

BUTTON NOSE

As we grow up, our face—including our nose—broadens and changes shape. But a baby's itty-bitty nose is cute as a, well, button.

ROLY-POLY BODY

Roll on! A baby grows super quickly and needs extra fat stores to keep her healthy. Meaning, she's got all the chub you need to love.

FLOPPY LIMBS

A baby's muscle tone takes months to develop, which is why newborns can't sit up on their own. This floppiness makes a baby seem more helpless—and stirs our desire to cuddle and protect her.

LARGE, ROUND HEAD

Big head? Just more to love. A newborn baby's head—which accounts for about 25 percent of her weight—is unusually large to accommodate a big brain relative to her body size.

BALD HEAD

No hair? No problem. A baby's lack of hair gives her a softer, rounder, more appealing appearance.

BIG FOREHEAD

A baby's skull can take up to 18 months to become fully formed. And because the bones aren't yet fused together, her forehead can be rounder and stick out a bit more than an adult's.

BIG EYES

What big eyes you have! By three months, a baby's eyes have reached their full adult width. So a little person's peepers look especially big—and endearing.

CHUBBY CHEEKS

A baby gets her round cheeks thanks to balls of fat called "sucking pads" that help her nurse or suck from a bottle.

INVITING SMILE

Try to resist the open, gummy grin of a kid—we dare you. Starting around six weeks old, a baby will show off "social smiles"—intentional expressions that display her happiness.

SMALL CHIN

A baby's chin is the perfect, petite point to her rounded face (even if it's covered in drool).

Babies' brains grow by one percent each day after birth.

Puppy
LOVE

JUST LIKE BABIES, puppies sure make people swoon! The natural response we have when spotting a little Lab or a mini mutt falls under the kinderschema philosophy described by Konrad Lorenz. Here are the features found on puppies that combine to make them so doggone cute.

Happy in a SNAP

Having a bad day? Look at a picture of a puppy! Scientists say that simply glancing at a snap of a sweet pooch can make you happy. Images of young dogs not only boost your mood, but they also can make you feel less aggressive and even improve your concentration. Talk about the power of a picture.

ROUND FACE

Much like in humans, a puppy's face is rounder than an adult dog's, making it more appealing.

LARGE HEAD

Not only does a puppy's oversize head increase its cuteness, researchers say that a dog's head tilt makes humans swoon.

BIG EYES

Who can resist puppy dog eyes? One study found that shelter dogs that widen their eyes and raise their inner brows find new homes faster.

BIG EARS

Most puppies grow into their features, but in the meantime, their oversize ears make these dogs even more darling.

SHORT SNOUT

Like a baby's button nose, a pup's nose and snout are stubbier than those of their adult counterparts.

LOOSE SKIN

Some breeds of dogs are born with extra skin, which will eventually tighten as they grow and develop more muscle. It's sure tough to resist those rolls!

FLOPPY LIMBS
Puppies take their first wobbly steps around 21 days old. Their clumsy gait makes them awfully cute.

BUNNY

ADORABLE ATTRIBUTE

Snub Nose

A more smooshed-in, shorter face than an older rabbit's boosts a baby bunny's appeal.

BABIES AND PUPPIES aren't the only adorable animals on Earth. Check out what makes other young creatures appear off-the-charts cute.

CUTE
by Nature

ELEPHANT CALF

ADORABLE ATTRIBUTE

Baby-Mom Bond

Scientists say that seeing these playful pachyderms hanging around their mamas reminds us of the bond humans have with our own moms.

GRIZZLY BEAR CUB

ADORABLE ATTRIBUTE

Big Head, Chubby Cheeks

It's no coincidence that the teddy bear is such a popular toy. An actual baby bear's big noggin and chubby cheeks make it a beloved animal around the world.

EMPEROR PENGUIN CHICK

ADORABLE ATTRIBUTE

Round Body

We are naturally drawn to emperor penguin chicks, with their plump bodies and fuzzy feathers.

BABY ORANGUTAN

ADORABLE ATTRIBUTE

Large Head and Eyes, Big Forehead

We go ape over the orangutan's prominent features. And who can resist that spiky tuft of hair?

TOO Cute!

Ever see something so cute you could just eat it up? You're not alone. Experts even have a name for this odd impulse: cute aggression. And, likely, the urge to squeal, screech, or even bite, squeeze, or eat something that's adorable is the result of our brain being overwhelmed with emotions—similar to why you may burst into tears of joy when something awesome happens. Good thing for us, when it comes to reacting to something cute, the brain quickly corrects itself before we can actually act on these emotions.

Your Brain ON CUTE

Sure, you love the look of babies. But when it comes to exactly *why* you think they're so adorable, there's a lot more to it than meets the eye. In fact, studies have shown that babies actually trigger a reaction in your brain that can cause the release of dopamine, the same feel-good chemical that's released when people fall in love. And experts say that seeing babies and puppies may tap into the parts of our brain associated with reward—resulting in that desire to be around cute things.

FAMILIAR FEATURES

So, what's going on in your body when you see a baby? First, your brain will recognize its endearing features—the wobbly head, the big eyes, the small nose and chubby cheeks. This triggers a reaction in the mesocorticolimbic system (the area in your brain associated with motivation and reward), causing a surge of dopamine throughout your system. The result? A satisfying feeling similar to munching on a cookie when you're craving something sweet.

SMELLS LIKE BABY

It's not always just the sight of a little one that can make us feel like smiling. One study showed that the natural smell of babies may trigger intense happiness—especially in new moms. Scientists observed that a whiff of pajamas previously worn by a newborn triggered the reward center of the brain among women who had recently given birth. Now, the scent of a dirty diaper may tell another story!

In Tagalog—a language spoken in the Philippines—the word *gigil* describes the **urge to pinch or squeeze** something that's extra adorable.

Survival OF THE CUTEST

Being cute isn't a requirement in life. But as a baby, it can certainly help you survive! As researcher Konrad Lorenz proposed more than 70 years ago, humans are hardwired to want to protect and care for babies—a theory that today's experts still support.

"Not only are babies cute, but they're harmless and helpless. They grab our attention quickly, and we have an evolutionary response to pay attention to them," says Joshua Dale, a professor of foreign languages and literature at Tokyo Gakugei University and an expert in the science of cute. "Cuteness is essential to survival."

Scientists say that most humans are biologically wired to find babies cute, harmless, and vulnerable, which explains why we have that natural urge to reach out and cuddle and care for them. This may be how some species survive.

This appeal applies to both baby humans and baby animals. Because our brain can't quite differentiate between the cuteness of a cooing baby or a sweet little kitten, both creatures can trigger a warm-and-fuzzy feeling—and that pull to provide and care for them. While experts aren't so sure if animals themselves have the same instincts, the theory may offer a biological explanation for why some species—mammals, especially—are so fiercely protective of their adorable offspring.

Humans with a **"baby face"** are thought to be more naive, helpless, kind, and warm than adults with more mature appearances.

CHAPTER 2

AWW-
some
ANIMALS!

WHAT'S THE MOST adorable animal on Earth? It's tough to pick just one! While some creatures are appealing for obvious reasons (hello, pudgy pandas and cuddly kittens), others are more, well, unconventionally cute. As you'll see in this chapter, cute can span all animal groups— from amphibians to arachnids (yep, that's right, even spiders!)— as well as both domesticated and wild species. Read on to take a look at the planet's most precious animals and explore more about what makes them just so darn lovable.

10

HEDGEHOG

DARLING DETAILS: Its small size and love of cuddling make this spiky mammal a perfect pet. And while those many quills (each hedgehog has up to 7,000 of them on top of its head and back) look fierce, this is a mostly cuddly critter, with soft fur on its face, legs, chest, and belly.

FUN FACT: A pet hedgehog named Azuki has more than 360,000 followers on Instagram.

Cute
COUNTDOWN

SOME ANIMALS simply have adorable in their DNA!
Here are 10 animals that are undeniably darling.

8

DOLPHIN

DARLING DETAILS: That friendly face and natural smile aren't the only things that make a dolphin stand out. Super smart and curious, the dolphin's playful personality makes it one of the most endearing animals in the ocean.

FUN FACT: A newborn dolphin is born with a tiny patch of hair on its chin.

CLOWNFISH

DARLING DETAILS: Nemo, is that you? This tropical fish may have gotten its fame from a movie, but the real-life version is just as appealing. And yes, it does live in an anemone, where it's protected from predators ... just like on the big screen.

FUN FACT: A female clownfish lays up to 1,000 eggs at a time.

9

7

HARP SEAL

DARLING DETAILS: With its irresistible face and fluffy fur, a harp seal is seriously sweet. Young seals are known for their snow-white pelt, which blends into the icy backgrounds of the Arctic and North Atlantic Oceans, where they live.

FUN FACT: Harp seal mothers are able to identify their babies by their smell.

CHAMELEON

DARLING DETAILS: What big eyes you have! A chameleon's prominent peepers give this reptile rockin' vision—it can spot a small bug some 30 feet (9 m) away.

FUN FACT: Chameleons can change their skin color in less than 20 seconds.

KOALA

DARLING DETAILS: No wonder a koala is so adorable—it gets plenty of beauty rest! In fact, this Australian native sleeps for as many as 22 hours a day. But it's not just being lazy. All that extra shut-eye helps the koala conserve energy—its steady diet of eucalyptus leaves doesn't provide much.

FUN FACT: Zookeepers working with baby koalas wrap them in blankets to make them feel like they're in a mother's pouch.

6

5

4
PIG

DARLING DETAILS: With its soft pink skin, floppy ears, and sturdy little body, a piglet definitely makes you squeal! And it's as clever as it is cute: A newborn pig learns to run to its mother's call, and those as young as six weeks can recognize their reflection in a mirror.

FUN FACT: Most piglets are born striped.

SEA TURTLE

DARLING DETAILS: Baby sea turtles are born with the odds stacked super high against them. Just 1 in 1,000 hatchlings will make it to adulthood, as they're vulnerable to everything from predators to rough seas. Which means it takes one tough turtle to survive.

FUN FACT: A baby sea turtle is born with a tiny temporary tooth on its snout that helps it break out of its shell.

2

RED-EYED TREE FROG

DARLING DETAILS: Wouldn't you like to just put this little hopper right in your pocket? But this frog's colorful look—especially its eyes—aren't just for show. If a hungry snake approaches, a sleeping frog can flash the bright red color and hopefully startle the predator. Then the frog, which lives in rain forests in southern Mexico and Central and South America, can safely hop away.

FUN FACT: Young red-eyed tree frogs are brown; they won't get their bright green skin until they're adults.

PYGMY HIPPO

DARLING DETAILS: While a pygmy hippo may look like its much bigger cousin, the smaller species spends a lot more time on land. Native to the forests and swamps of West Africa, this mammal sweats a pink ooze, which naturally cools the animal in its hot and humid surroundings.

FUN FACT: At birth, a pygmy hippo weighs about the same as a newborn human baby.

1

PENGUIN

ADORABLE ADAPTATION:
Waddly walk

CUTE, DECODED: Despite their side-to-side shuffle, penguins don't need better balance. Experts believe their characteristic wobble is more efficient than a regular walk, since they're able to transfer extra energy back and forth with each waddle, like a swinging pendulum. And that extra energy is key for helping penguins stay strong during their long, icy migrations.

Conventionally CUTE

JUST WHAT IS that special something that makes a critter so cute? Sometimes, nature has made them that way so they have a better chance to survive in the wild. Here, we decode the science behind some animals' most adorable adaptations.

CHIPMUNK

ADORABLE ADAPTATION: Chubby cheeks

CUTE, DECODED: Those cheeks may be cute, but they're quite useful, too. Pouches on each side of a chipmunk's mouth—which can stretch up to three times the size of its head—are like grocery bags the little rodents can stuff with food like berries, seeds, and grains. In just a few days, chipmunks can stockpile enough food to get them through an entire winter. So cheeky!

GIANT PANDA

ADORABLE ADAPTATION:
Black eye patches

CUTE, DECODED: We love the look of those black rings around a panda's eyes, but those aren't just for show. Experts say that the patches may have evolved to protect pandas from predators, as they make their eyes appear 10 times bigger than they actually are. The patches also help pandas recognize one another.

TARSIER

ADORABLE ADAPTATION: Huge eyes

CUTE, DECODED: Peepers as big as Ping-Pong balls give this primate an eye-popping, animated appearance. The nocturnal tarsier's eyes actually assist it at night when it is hunting for food—or watching out for predators.

PUPPY

ADORABLE ADAPTATION: Extra-soft fur

CUTE, DECODED: All dogs are born with supersoft, fuzzy fur, also known as a puppy coat. This fur serves as a protective layer for their brand-new skin and helps regulate body temperature. Within a few months, the adult coat grows in, which is thicker, stiffer, and better suited for the outdoors.

WALRUS

ADORABLE ADAPTATION: Round body and rolls

CUTE, DECODED: At around 2,200 pounds (1,000 kg), there's a lot to love when it comes to an adult walrus. But its chunky body has little to do with its diet—although it does eat up to 50 pounds (23 kg) of food per day. All of that blubber—which can measure up to six inches (15 cm) thick—actually keeps a walrus's body temp about 1.8 to 5.4°F (1 to 3°C) warmer than the water, meaning these animals don't have to worry about developing frostbite in frigid seas.

FENNEC FOX

ADORABLE ADAPTATION: Extra-large ears

CUTE, DECODED: Bigger ears, better hearing? In the case of fennec foxes, their oversize organs do give them a boost when it comes to listening for bugs—they can even pick up on the sound of critters crawling underground! And because both ears are packed with blood vessels, the foxes are better equipped to radiate body heat, helping them stay cool in the hot desert.

Unconventionally CUTE

ALL CREATURES great and small are beautiful in their own way. But there are some animals that are often cast off as anything but adorable. With blobby bodies, peculiar appendages, and spiky skin, their appearance can be more startling than sweet. Still, you can't help but love them—funky features and all. Here's a roundup of animals that are just so ugly, they're cute!

HOLY MOLE-Y

There's just something about the **European mole's** piglike snout and explosion of whiskers that make these reclusive rodents appealing. And they may be tiny, but they're mighty strong, able to lift 20 times their own body weight.

WINNING GRIN

Bet you can't keep a straight face when looking at this smiley salamander! The rare **axolotl**—found only in a certain part of Mexico—exhibits a rare phenomenon called neoteny, which means it will always look the same as it did as a tadpole. So even as an axolotl grows older, it'll never lose its baby face.

MASHUP MAMMAL

The **platypus** has a duck's bill and webbed feet, a beaver's fur, and an otter's tail. Oh, and the females lay eggs, too. The platypus is so peculiar that the first scientists to examine a specimen thought it might have been a hoax because they'd never seen anything like it. But despite all of its quirks, you can't deny that this hodgepodge animal is actually endearing, in a wacky sort of way.

BIG MOUTH

Frog ... or hippo? With a massive mouth relative to its size, the **Budgett's frog** bears a strong resemblance to the equally bigmouthed mammal. Its cartoonlike appearance and blob of a body may make it look harmless, but watch out: This frog is a fierce hunter and is known to scream when threatened.

STICK IT

There's not much *not* to love about the **lumpsucker fish.** Besides its LOL-worthy name, the lumpsucker has a perfectly round body. Because of its body shape and tiny fins, this itty-bitty fish has trouble staying upright. So it anchors itself to rocks and coral with a built-in suction beneath its pelvic fin. Now that's some stick-to-itiveness.

Defending Ugly **ANIMALS**

No one wants to see any animal go extinct. But one study showed that when it comes to conservation efforts, classically cute animals—think tigers, pandas, chimps, and elephants—get more love. Case in point? Scientists publish about 500 times more papers about mammals than amphibians—while reptiles, birds, and small mammals get even less love. In a span of 20 years, various researchers published 100 studies on meerkats, while lumpy (but lovable) manatees were featured in just 14 papers.

Fortunately, people are stepping up to ensure that every animal gets the attention it deserves. For example, a team in New Zealand is focusing on saving a smelly mouse-size cricket called a weta (which means "god of ugly things" in the indigenous Maori language) from extinction. And organizations like the Ugly Animal Preservation Society are speaking up for those species that are often overshadowed by more conventionally cute and cuddly critters. The goal? To remind people that *all* animals need to be protected.

CUTE CRAWLERS

INSECTS AND SPIDERS are often the last critters to be considered cute. Why? According to research, they lack the classic appealing features, like an animated face, plump body, or chubby cheeks. But there are some exceptions to the rule. Here are some bugs that are more cute-crawly than creepy-crawly.

POODLE MOTH

WHERE IT LIVES: Venezuela

WHY IT'S CUTE: Covered with fuzzy white fur, this recently discovered moth is named for its resemblance to the curly-haired dog. Its fur is used to protect it from predators and can irritate your skin, making it far less cuddly than an actual poodle.

LADYBUG

WHERE IT LIVES: Worldwide

WHY IT'S CUTE: With its bright red coloring and polka-dot pattern (meant to scare off predators), the ladybug is loved around the world. They're thought to be a sign of good luck, and they are also used by farmers as a safe alternative to pesticides because they feast on plant-eating insects, such as aphids.

HAPPY FACE SPIDER

WHERE IT LIVES: The islands of Oahu, Molokai, Maui, and Hawaii

WHY IT'S CUTE: This spider doesn't need a smiley face emoji to let you know how it's feeling—just look at its back! This small spider—tinier than your pinkie nail—has a distinctive marking that experts believe actually evolved to confuse birds and other foes.

DAMSELFLY

WHERE IT LIVES:
Worldwide

WHY IT'S CUTE:
With the damselfly, the eyes have it—all five of them! With two huge, spaced-out peepers plus another three eyes on top, this smaller relative of the dragonfly has a look that will make you smile!

BEE FLY

WHERE IT LIVES: Japan

WHY IT'S CUTE: This tiny flier is actually the inspiration for the Pokémon character Cutiefly. It's not actually a bee—it's part of the fly family. And while it doesn't sting, it does feed on flower nectar like its buzzing buddies.

WOOLLY BEAR CATERPILLAR

WHERE IT LIVES: United States and southern Canada

WHY IT'S CUTE: Bad hair day? With its wild coif, this fuzzy fella could give Albert Einstein a run for his money. The caterpillar—the larval form of the tiger moth—really gets around. In fact, it travels up to a mile (1.6 km) a day, snacking on a variety of plants.

Sweet FEET

Paws down, these tiny feet are totally adorable. And they actually belong to a spider! Turns out, some spiders' hairy feet—also known as claw tufts—look a lot like a cat's or dog's paws. And these feet aren't just cute—they're super helpful, too. These tiny claws help spiders cling to webs and walls, and some spiders even use their feet to hear, smell, and navigate their way back home.

CHAPTER 3

NO MATTER WHERE you're from, the language of cute is universal. But where you live may have a lot to do with how much of your world revolves around adorable things. Take, for example, Japan, the birthplace of cute culture. In Tokyo, you can't walk a city block without seeing something that'll make you say "aww." Read on and explore more about how the power of cute spans the globe!

Cute
AROUND THE
WORLD!

In Japan, people are so crazy about cute stuff that there's even a name to describe their love of lovable things: "Kawaii." While its literal translation means "able to be loved," Kawaii is a catch-all term used for anything adorable, sweet, innocent, and pure. And in Japan, especially, Kawaii is king.

IT'S IN THE WRITING

Kawaii may seem totally trendy, but it's not a new phenomenon. In fact, the term was first used in the 1970s, when teenage girls began using rounder, more childlike handwriting (some say they were inspired by a certain font used in comic books). The teens also wrote horizontally—not vertically like traditional Japanese—and added emoticons like little animals, hearts, and stars to their writing. While "kitten writing" was often frowned upon (some schools even banned kids from using it), the new handwriting eventually became the norm and snowballed into cute-ifying other everyday things, from fashion to food to household appliances and even construction barriers. And it's only gotten more adorable since.

KAWAII EVERYWHERE

Japan has a firm grip on Kawaii culture, but its influence has certainly spread around the world. Today, you can see the impact in things like selfie filters on social media, in the popularity of emojis and bitmojis, and in anime shows and graphic novels. And take a look at Hello Kitty: Thirty years after emerging from the early Kawaii movement in Japan, it's now a worldwide, beloved multibillion-dollar brand.

FOREVER CUTE

So what's the secret to Kawaii's lasting power? For starters, it triggers our natural biological response to covet all things cute. And it affects our emotions, too: As people grow older and get more responsibilities, Kawaii can make an adult feel like a kid again. After all, who doesn't love to add emojis to their text messages or pop a pair of dog ears on their selfies? Cute never gets old. And that, experts say, is why Kawaii is here to stay.

Kawaii
EVERYWHERE

The *Oxford English Dictionary* named the "Face With Tears of Joy" **emoji** its 2015 Word of the Year.

ALL KINDS OF Kawaii

FROM SCHOOL SUPPLIES to traffic cones, Kawaii is just about everywhere you look. Here are nine examples of how this irresistibly cute trend crops up in everyday life.

CONSTRUCTION BARRIERS

Move over, basic orange cones: On some Japanese city streets, construction barriers appear as colorful figures like bunnies and monkeys.

MANHOLE COVERS

Look down! Some 12,000 decorated manhole covers can be found throughout Japan. The darling designs are so popular that they even have their own trading cards.

WASHI TAPE

No wonder washi tape is, uh, sticking around: This colorful crafting supply is made from washi paper—a traditional Japanese paper—and features all sorts of delightful designs.

MASCOTS

Japanese towns, cities, airports, and even prisons are each represented by a mascot, also known as a *yuru-kyara*. Every year, these yuru-kyara make their way to an annual grand prix, where one character is named Mascot of the Year based on a popular vote.

PENS

Write on! Colorful pens with tiny toppers in the shape of your favorite things (yum, doughnuts!) make taking notes a novelty!

STICKY NOTES

You can't ignore important reminders when they're jotted down on neat notes in the shape of adorable animals like polar bears and pufferfish.

CARNIVAL RIDES

Whee! Amusement park rides are even more fun when you get to share the thrills with your favorite cartoon characters like Hello Kitty.

PENCIL SHARPENER

Both your pencils and your classroom style will be on point when you keep a colorful duck or elephant sharpener in your school supply stash.

TOILET PAPER

Are you sure you want to flush that? Not only is this TP totally adorable, but it's scented, too!

WASHI TAPE

MANHOLE COVER

MASCOTS

CONSTRUCTION BARRIERS

GOLD MEDAL Mascots

MASCOTS MAY RULE in Japan, but cuddly characters have made their mark around the world—especially at the Olympics. Meant to serve as playful ambassadors for the host country and to get kids excited about the games, these mascots—which have ranged from animals to ice cubes—have made appearances at the Olympics since 1968. Read on to find out more about the most adorable Olympic mascots through the years.

CALGARY, 1988

The Mascots: **Hidy and Howdy**

AWW-SOME INFO: Who doesn't love a pair of polar bears in cowboy hats? The arctic bears were chosen for their cuddle factor, while the cowboy gear represented Calgary's country-western flair.

MUNICH, 1972

The Mascot: **Waldi**

AWW-SOME INFO: This colorful dachshund—a popular breed in Germany at the time—was the first official Olympic mascot. His original design came about at a holiday party for the Munich Games Organising Committee, at which attendees submitted ideas using crayons and clay.

INNSBRUCK, 1976

The Mascot: **Schneemandl**

AWW-SOME INFO: Before there was Olaf, there was Schneemandl, the lovable snowman that made headlines as the first ever official Winter Games mascot. As for that red hat? It was reflective of the style worn by people in that region of Austria at the time.

BARCELONA, 1992

The Mascot: **Cobi**

AWW-SOME INFO: One of the most abstract mascots ever, Cobi is actually a Pyrenean mountain dog depicted in Cubism, an art style originated by Spaniard Pablo Picasso. Cobi's looks might have been unconventional, but his appeal was undeniable—he even starred in his own cartoon series.

ATLANTA, 1996

The Mascot: **Izzy**

AWW-SOME INFO: What's in a name? Plenty—if you're an Olympic mascot. Initially called Whatzit because it's not an animal, a person, or an object, the name Izzy was voted on by Atlanta schoolkids, who also helped with its design.

BEIJING, 2008

The Mascots: **Beibei, Jingjing, Yingying, Nini, Huanhuan**

AWW-SOME INFO: This cute crew—also known as the Fuwa—repped a range of cherished Chinese symbols and animals, including the panda (Jingjing) and the Tibetan antelope (Yingying). Each of their names rhymes by repeating the same syllable, a traditional Chinese way of showing love to kids.

VANCOUVER, 2010

The Mascot: **Quatchi**

AWW-SOME INFO: Short for "Sasquatch," Quatchi brought a sweeter spin to the legendary furry creature said to lurk in nearby forests. He was often accompanied by his co-mascot Miga, a made-up animal called a sea bear that was part killer whale and part Kermode bear.

PYEONGCHANG, 2018

The Mascot: **Soohorang**

AWW-SOME INFO: All eyes were on this friendly feline at South Korea's Winter Games. An animal deeply rooted in Korean mythology, the white tiger was also said to be a protective pal to all athletes in the games. Nice!

HE'S ABOUT AS TALL as a 12-year-old, with a round belly, two bright red circles for cheeks, a big smile, and wide eyes. His arms are always outstretched, as if ready to wrap someone in a hug at any minute. He's adorable, undoubtedly adored—and all over the place. This is Kumamon, the official mascot of Kumamoto Prefecture, an area of about 1.85 million people. And while Kumamon may represent just one part of Japan, he's quickly become one of the most recognized mascots on Earth. Here's more about this beloved bear.

MEET
Kumamon

1 HE'S RICH. In one year alone, Kumamon's merchandise—everything from clothes to key chains to bags of carrots—earned about $1.15 billion for Kumamoto. His products are so popular that a stuffed Kumamon bear once sold out in just five seconds—for $276 a pop.

2 HE'S REALLY BUSY. Kumamon makes about 2,000 appearances every year and has traveled as far as France and Massachusetts, U.S.A. He's met Japan's imperial couple and has walked the red carpet at movie premieres.

3 HE'S BIG ON SOCIAL MEDIA. More than 111,000 fans follow Kumamon's comings and goings on Twitter, where he posts updates on his activities and plenty of silly snaps. A video of him dancing has more than three million hits on YouTube.

4 HE RIDES A MOTORCYCLE. After Kumamon was seen riding a mini motorcycle made for him (and yes, he wore a helmet!), sales of the bike skyrocketed.

5 HE FLIES THE FRIENDLY SKIES. In 2016, one airline began flying planes with Kumamon's image painted on them. The planes, based in Kyushu and Okinawa, fly to major cities in Japan.

6 HE'S A RUNNER. Each year, runners try to beat the bear at his own 5K (3.1-mile) race in Thailand. Kumamon is also a regular cheerleader on the sidelines of marathons and other running events throughout Japan, as well as other parts of Asia.

7 HE'S MISCHIEVOUS. Kumamon isn't just loved for his cute looks. He's also known to have a bit of a naughty streak, once "escaping" to the city of Osaka (actually a publicity stunt to get people to take the train from Kumamoto to look for him, which worked).

8 HE'S THE BOSS. Since 2014, Kumamon has been considered the "director of public relations" of Kumamoto, a nod to his role in appearing in many tourist campaigns and traveling with the governor.

9 HE LIKES TO PARTY. Every March 12, Kumamoto celebrates its mascot's official birthday with a bang. Past parties have included multiday festivals featuring parades, a huge cake, and presents.

10 HE'S AS GOOD AS GOLD.
One of those birthday gifts? A seven-inch (17-cm) Kumamon figurine made out of pure gold crafted by a local jeweler. The shiny statue went on sale for about $1 million.

AFRICA

WHAT: Goat Tower

WHERE:
Paarl, South Africa

WHY IT'S CUTE: Goats steal the show at this working farm, where guests can watch the local residents hoof up and down a two-story spiral staircase and cross an arching sky-bridge. Head there in September and you can cuddle with the new crop of kids welcomed by the nanny goats each year.

ANTARCTICA

WHAT: Paradise Harbor

WHERE: Antarctica

WHY IT'S CUTE: This penguin playground—accessible only by boat—is the perfect place to peek at the Arctic birds. Watch gentoo penguins slide on their bellies in the ice or waddle around on ice floes. If you make it to land, some of the more curious creatures may make their way toward you.

CUTE ON EVERY CONTINENT

7 Adorable tourist attractions around the world

AUSTRALIA

WHAT: Gnomesville

WHERE: Wellington Mill, Australia

WHY IT'S CUTE: Thousands of garden gnomes gather at this parcel of parkland in Australia. In 1999, a local resident placed a single gnome in the hollow of a tree, starting a trend that eventually turned into an entire village of the bearded figurines.

ASIA

WHAT: Teddy Bear Museum

WHERE: Jeju Island, South Korea

WHY IT'S CUTE: Get up close and cuddly with stuffed bears in every shape, size—and outfit. See bears dressed up as everyone from Elvis Presley to the Beatles to Mona Lisa. There's even an exhibit staging the first landing on the moon. It's almost un*bear*ably adorable.

EUROPE

WHAT: Miffy Museum

WHERE: Utrecht, the Netherlands

WHY IT'S CUTE: Miffy may have appeared in her first book in 1955, but this bunny is as popular as ever. With 10 colorful rooms dedicated to the cute white rabbit, this museum is a blast for kids of all ages.

NORTH AMERICA

WHAT: The Amazing World of Dr. Seuss Museum

WHERE: Springfield, Massachusetts, U.S.A.

WHY IT'S CUTE: In this first and only museum dedicated to Theodor Geisel (aka Dr. Seuss), the playful pages of his beloved books come to life in every exhibit. Take a tour through Readingville, check out Geisel's collection of playful hats, or stroll through a sculpture garden featuring favorite characters like the Lorax and the Cat in the Hat.

SOUTH AMERICA

WHAT: Paddington Bear of Lima

WHERE: Lima, Peru

WHY IT'S CUTE: From London to Lima, Paddington Bear sure gets around! This sweet statue of Paddington dressed up in his finest traveling clothes was a gift to Peru from the British Embassy as a nod to the fictional bear's birthplace.

IT'S a SMALL World

THESE SCALED-DOWN setups of famous places bring new meaning to the phrase "world wonders."

OUT OF THIS WORLD

GULLIVER'S GATE • New York City

You can travel around the world in just a few minutes with a visit to Gulliver's Gate, a $40 million art exhibit in New York City. A team of more than 100 artists and engineers used 3D printing, laser cutting, and a lot of hard work to reproduce several of the world's **major cities** across five continents. With running water and working electricity, these mini cities buzz just as they do in real life, with features like flashing billboards in Times Square, flowing waterfalls, and a replica of the Panama Canal complete with a working lock that allows boats to sail through.

LITTLE VILLAGE

VILLAGE OF LOWER CRACKPOT • Promised Land, Australia

Tiny houses have taken over this peculiar park in **Tasmania,** where you'll find a miniature village built to one-fifth scale. While most of the buildings honor Australia's culture and history (like a church decorated with the Aboriginal flag), you'll also spy some small versions of popular international sites, including the Eiffel Tower.

COMPACT CONTINENT

MINI-EUROPE • Brussels, Belgium

From a (not so) Big Ben to a compact Colosseum, this park places you right in the heart of Europe: **350** of the continent's coolest attractions have been made miniature, some even featuring interactive effects like an erupting Mount Vesuvius in Italy.

MODEL CITIZENS

MINI ISRAEL PARK • Latrun, Israel

At this adorable attraction, the entire country of Israel fits into a space the size of some seven soccer fields. Check out nearly 400 replicas of Israel's most iconic landmarks, like Jerusalem's **Western Wall**, Mount Hermon, and the skyscrapers of Tel Aviv—all scaled down to 1/25 of their actual size. The shrunken scenarios also feature 25,000 Shopkin-size residents and an airport with petite planes taxiing on the runway.

NO SMALL FEAT

STANLEY MINIVENTURES • Bangkok, Thailand

Said to be the "biggest little world" in Asia, this impressive layout offers **11** distinct and diminutive areas. Peer into an organic farm, a mini Chinatown, a working replica of the Hoover Dam, and the Swiss Alps, all scaled down to 1/87 of their size in real life.

Mini but MIGHTY

For centuries, humans have been mad about making things mini. So what's the appeal of these tiny towns, specifically? Experts say that not only are small-scale models fun to look at, but they expand and engage our imaginations—a proven way to boost happiness. Also, in a time when life seems nonstop and sometimes out of our control, gazing into a miniature world can give you a sense of power that increases confidence. Now you know how King Kong must've felt when he took over New York City.

CHAPTER 4

SO CUTE
(YOU CAN EAT IT!)

 YOU SIT DOWN for lunch and are given two options to eat. On one plate: a plain ol' peanut butter and jelly sandwich with apple slices. On the other? Another PB&J, but the bread is cut into a star shape, and the apple slices are arranged like a smiley face. The food on each plate is exactly the same—yet you're more likely to reach for the "cute" arrangement, right?

Turns out, the cuter the food, the more likely we are to eat it. One study supports this fact, saying that indulging in "playful" products, including food, is much more rewarding and enjoyable than opting for run-of-the-mill meals. And folks in the food industry—from bakers to farmers to restaurant owners—have picked up on this trend. Feast your eyes on the different ways cute food has become something just about everyone wants to take a bite out of.

CUTE Fruit
(AND VEGGIES, TOO!)

EATING THE healthy stuff isn't such a chore when the veggies and fruit are this fun! Here are top picks for precious produce.

KIWI BERRIES

Size isn't the only thing that these "ki-wees" have in common with grapes. Because they lack the fuzzy skin of their larger cousin, you can snack on these sweet fruits like grapes, too.

FUN FACT: *Kiwis are sometimes known as Chinese gooseberries.*

HEART-SHAPED POTATO

You can't help but, uh, heart this peculiar potato. This shape is the result of the potato's stem swelling and splitting in two at the base but not separating. Eventually, the spud grows into the symbol of love.

FUN FACT: *Oddly shaped potatoes are often turned into french fries instead of being sold in stores.*

BUDDHA PEAR

These may look like something out of a fairy tale, but these pudgy pears are the real deal. Thanks to a special mold placed on a pear when it's just starting to grow, the fruit eventually takes the shape of the cherished spiritual figure. Similar molds are used to produce square watermelons and soccer ball–shaped gourds.

FUN FACT: *When sold in stores, funky-shaped fruit can cost up to three times as much as regular produce.*

48

PINK PINEAPPLES

The flesh of this fabulous pineapple, nicknamed the Rosé, is pink, thanks to the addition of lycopene—the same pigment that makes tomatoes red and gives watermelons their rosy hue. As if their color isn't appealing enough, these pineapples are also engineered to be extra sweet.

FUN FACT: *Pineapple plants produce pink and purple flowers.*

BABY ARTICHOKES

Despite their name, these artichokes are actually all grown up. They're just smaller (but still fully mature) versions of larger globe artichokes and even bloom on the same plant. Because they're situated lower and away from the sun, they stay small—and taste slightly sweeter.

FUN FACT: *Artichokes are edible flower buds.*

MOUSE MELONS

Also known as a cucamelon, or *sandita* in Spanish, these fruits are smaller than a Ping-Pong ball and look like mini watermelons but actually taste like cucumber and lime.

FUN FACT: *Mouse melons grow on vines.*

TOMATOES

SCIENCE TO Grow ON

HOW DOES your garden grow? In the case of heart-shaped potatoes or baby artichokes, the cute comes naturally. But mostly, when it comes to super-specialized produce, there's plenty of science involved before they sprout.

CROSSING CROPS

Sometimes, harvesting adorable fruits and veggies is simply about selective breeding. Growers will cross the seeds of smaller and smaller plants until they come up with a cute crop like snack-size BellaFina bell peppers or baby broccoli, which is a cross between broccoli and Chinese kale. This plant-breeding technique is also used to come up with fun fruit hybrids, like pluots and peacharines. Kalette, a cross between kale and brussels sprouts, recently hit produce stands as a flavorful blend of the two veggies—and it just so happens to look like a mini head of dark green lettuce.

TEST LAB

And then there's genetic engineering—or using modern biotechnology to make changes to a plant's genetic makeup and give it a preferred trait. Pineapples contain both pink pigment (lycopene) and yellow pigment (beta-carotene). To get the pink hue, scientists lowered the enzymes in the standard pineapple that transform the naturally occurring pink pigment to yellow pigment. And scientists in Britain are developing a tomato with dark purple pigment, which is said to give the fruit an extra boost of cancer-fighting antioxidants.

THE FUTURE OF FRUIT

Scientists are using similar processes to enhance other fruits and veggies, like the Arctic apple, which is slower to brown when exposed to open air than a regular apple. They've also come up with funky flavors, such as cotton candy grapes, said to taste like spun sugar. The use of science to modify nature will always be up for debate, but it sure makes you wonder: What wild and crazy shapes and sizes will we see in veggies and fruit in the future?

BROCCOLI

BABY BROCCOLI

PLUMS + APRICOTS = PLUOTS

KALE

KALETTE

It took scientists 15 years to perfect **kalette.**

(REALLY)

Hungry? Too bad!
Mini meals won't fill you up—but they sure are adorable! Here's a look into the tiny food trend.

A plate no bigger than a penny piled with spaghetti. A ham sandwich the size of a vitamin. Burgers you can balance on your fingertip. Nope, these aren't dinners for a dollhouse family: They are actual bite-size concoctions created by real-life chefs. And not only are these adorable edibles Instagram-worthy, they're mostly made from scratch, too.

SMALL BEGINNINGS
So what's behind the miniature food movement? It all started in Japan (surprise!), where tiny things totally rule (see page 34 for much more about the cute culture there). A couple of years back, pictures of tiny culinary creations—first made from clay and then actual food—began popping up on social media from Asia. Creative chefs and artists from around the world followed suit, and now, millions of people a day check out YouTube channels and social media accounts dedicated to dainty dining.

BRAIN CANDY
The popularity of tiny food isn't all that surprising. After all, what's not to like about a stack of teensy pancakes topped with the most petite pat of butter you've ever seen? Experts say that admiring adorable food taps into the reward system in our brain. Just looking at tiny things, whether food or a baby animal, fills us with feel-good vibes much like a good meal fills our bellies and keeps us satisfied (for a little while at least!). Plus, the how-to videos are just plain fun—and a bit mesmerizing. "There's an appeal to watching tiny food being made by a pair of hands in a tiny kitchen," says Oren Katzeff, head of programming at Tastemade, a global digital food network that produces the super-popular Tiny Kitchen videos. "Everything is tiny from start to finish, and that's unexpected and delightful."

PLATES

The world's smallest restaurant serves just **two people** at a time.

MAKE MINE A Mini

NO DOUBT about it, the tiny food trend is taking off! Since this food frenzy started in Japan, people from all over the planet have been pining for these pint-size meals. Clips of chefs putting together these dainty dishes have generated millions of clicks and likes online and attracted thousands of visitors hungry for a taste of these mini meals. Hungry for more? Check out these takes on tiny plates from Tastemade.

Food Fake OUT

These itty-bitty bites may look delicious, but you wouldn't want to actually eat them! Artists like Stephanie Kilgast use polymer clay to whip up fake food to be used in dollhouses or as jewelry or collector's items. From a tray full of breakfast goodies (complete with a mini mug of coffee!) to dainty dumplings, Kilgast's creations are all about 1/12 the size of the actual items they're inspired by. While they may be small, these sculptures attract a huge audience: Kilgast has more than 100,000 followers on Instagram and some of her clay confections can fetch up to $700 a piece!

BREAKFAST

LUNCH

DINNER

DESSERT

SNACK

COOKING UP Cute

CUT TO SIZE

Ingredients like fruit, vegetables, and bread are cut down to size to match the scale of the small plates.

Tastemade

INGREDIENTS

Tiny cooks look for smaller swaps of actual ingredients, like quail eggs instead of a chicken eggs, or petite pearl onions instead of full-size onions.

A look inside an actual TINY kitchen

IT'S ONE THING to create micro-meals in your own kitchen, but true tiny food fanatics (also known as miniacs) cook over stoves small enough to fit in a dollhouse. Here's a look inside a tiny Tastemade kitchen, where the mini magic happens.

UTENSILS

All of the utensils—from the spatula to knives to the mini mixers—are tiny versions of the actual items.

CABINETS

The kitchen itself is literally a scaled-down version of a big one, even down to the cupboards.

STOVE/BURNER

The burner, heated by a tea candle, is hot enough to fry oil and heat a pan. Water in a supersmall pot boils in about two minutes. An itty-bitty burger can be cooked through in just a minute on each side.

TIME FOR PIZZA

Tiny Kitchen chefs recently whipped up a pepperoni pizza that was about the same size as a quarter.

Tastemade has over 12 seasons of Tiny Kitchen cooking online.

COOKING CLASS

It takes up to three hours to produce a 90-second tiny food cooking video.

THE CREATOR

Set pieces are made by artisans (oftentimes dollhouse makers) from all over the world, including England and Germany.

THE CHEFS

A chef rewrites existing recipes to adapt them to mini serving sizes.

Bean Sprouts

WHERE: U.S.A.

WHY IT'S CUTE: At this kid-focused restaurant, menu options called Imaginibbles make eating healthy food fun. Try the Taste Buds (chicken and veggie wrap), Crocamole (avocado hummus and veggie dippers), then finish off your meal with Pea-moji cookies. Yum!

ADORABLE
Dining Experiences

THESE CHARMING restaurants serve up a heaping dose of the warm and fuzzies!

Giraffe Manor

WHERE: Nairobi, Kenya

WHY IT'S CUTE: Love giraffes? Then you'll adore this breakfast room, part of a large hotel set on a 140-acre (57-ha) forest. There, a herd of Rothschild's giraffes roam freely—and are known to poke their heads through the restaurant's windows seeking a snack while you eat.

Meow Parlour

WHERE: New York, New York, U.S.A.

WHY IT'S CUTE: At this cat-themed café, munch on kitty-shaped cookies as cats—which are all available for adoption—roam free. Check out a Yoga & Kitties class, or just hang out and sip on a warm drink while a cat curls up in your lap. Sounds *purrfect*.

Hello Kitty Grand Cafe

WHERE: Irvine, California, U.S.A.

WHY IT'S CUTE: Hello Kitty rules at this cute café, where everything from the menu to the darling decor is dedicated to the famous icon and her sweet Sanrio friends.

Pudding Coffee Shop

WHERE: Barcelona, Spain

WHY IT'S CUTE: Kids rule at this café, where whimsical decorations, like tall toadstools and colorful murals on the walls, make you feel like you're dining in a wonderland.

Moomin House Café

WHERE: Tokyo, Japan

WHY IT'S CUTE: No one ever has to worry about eating alone at this quirky café, where diners are offered stuffed animal companions named Moomins. The hope? That no one leaves hungry—or lonely.

SO-O-O Sweet!

GET A TASTE
of these eight desserts that are as darling as they are delicious.

CONFECTION PURRFECTION

Sweets artist Laura from Japan draws inspiration from her real-life kitty, Apelila, to come up with cat-themed treats, like this sweet scene made from ingredients including modeling chocolate, sugar paste, and truffles. *Meeow.*

PENGUIN PUFF

This penguin is prepared for the elements! A pastry chef at Dominique Ansel Bakery in London, England, created this double-decker cream puff, filled with Mexican hot chocolate cream with a hint of chili powder. So cool.

GO FISH

In case eating ice cream out of a bowl isn't, well, cool enough, now you can enjoy your soft-serve straight out of a fish-shaped waffle cone. Also known as *taiyaki,* this cone is a spin-off of the traditional Japanese dessert of a fish-shaped cake filled with sweet red bean paste.

HEY, MICKEY

Exclusively served in Disney World, this dessert—two pumpkin-flavored waffles alongside vanilla ice cream, whipped cream, sprinkles, and caramel sauce—is a fitting treat for the Happiest Place on Earth.

MAGICALLY DELICIOUS

You don't have to go to the land of make-believe to sip on unicorn hot chocolate, a whimsical version of the wintry favorite. Topped with rainbow bursts of whipped cream, sprinkles, and marshmallows, this drink is as legendary as the one-horned horse it's named after.

THANKS A LATTE

A coffee shop in Hong Kong takes latte art to the next level. Made with foamed milk and enhanced by all-natural food coloring, 3D creatures like cats, pigs, and even an octopus have topped customers' cups of coffee. Adding to the adorableness? The fluffy foamy friends are meant to wiggle when you gently shake the cup.

PRETTY TASTY

Cute confections—also known as *wagashi*—are big in Japan. Bite-size sweets have been accompanying the traditional Japanese tea ceremony for centuries, and today's pastry chefs outdo themselves to create the most darling desserts and turn them into art you can eat.

PIECE OF PIE

Tiny pies are perfect when you want just one slice. And in flavors like peach, double chocolate cream, and key lime, they bring big flavor in every little bite.

CHAPTER 5

THE BUSINESS OF Cute

 NO QUESTION, cute sells. As humans, we are naturally attracted to sweet and cuddly things. And just like we are more likely to reach for that sandwich that's been stylized to look like a butterfly than the one with basic bread, we're also inclined to open our wallets for extra-cute clothes, toys, and other everyday items. Over the years, the business world has picked up on the power of cute. The result? Adorable ads and precious products that are hard to resist. Read on to find out more about how businesses have cashed in on cute.

ADORABLE Icons

ADORABLE THINGS can attract our attention in an instant. So it's no surprise that companies have used charming characters to market their products over the years. Here's how certain brands have banked on cute to sell their stuff.

😊 1898 😊
MICHELIN MAN

WHY IT WORKS: Inspired by a stack of tires, this lovable personality has been tied to one of the world's best-selling tire brands for more than a century. His popularity has grown over the years, and he has evolved with the times. In 2017 he received a makeover, becoming more svelte and lighter, while conserving his legendary warmth.

😊 1914 😊
MORTON SALT GIRL®

WHY IT WORKS: This eight-year-old has been an icon in the ad world for more than a century. Her rainy-day gear, including her big umbrella, bright yellow dress, and open carton of salt, was initially meant to market salt that doesn't clump in wet or humid weather.

😊 1953 😊
COPPERTONE GIRL

WHY IT WORKS: The, um, *cheeky* image of a puppy nipping a young girl's bathing suit has tugged on heartstrings to sell sunscreen for more than 65 years. The original sketch—which later appeared on billboards and magazines and remains on Coppertone packaging today—was modeled after an actual three-year-old by her artist mom.

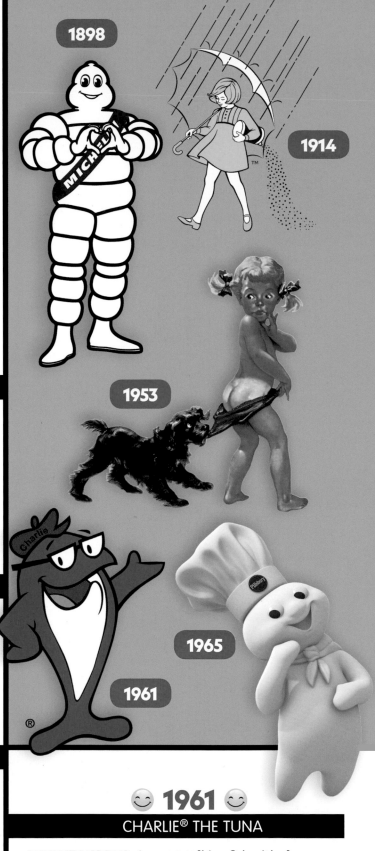

😊 1961 😊
CHARLIE® THE TUNA

WHY IT WORKS: A smart-talking fish with glasses may not be the first thing you think of as an advertising icon, but Charlie® has helped make StarKist® one of the best-selling brands of tuna. The famous catchphrase "Sorry, Charlie" was actually created for the commercials.

SNUGGLE BEAR

WHY IT WORKS: The adorable spokes-bear aimed to "make the world a softer place" as the mascot for Snuggle fabric softener. In ads, he has jumped out of laundry baskets and lived up to his name by cuddling everything from towels to T-shirts. After all these years, Snuggle Bear's mission is still enabling families to create snuggle-up moments.

😊 1989 😊

ENERGIZER BUNNY™

WHY IT WORKS: It keeps going and going and ... The hot-pink, shades-wearing, drum-playing rabbit has become such an adored icon that, according to a 2008 study, a whopping 95 percent of people recognize it. And it's not just the commercials people are crazy about: In 2010, headlines reported that one of the original Energizer Bunny™ toys sold for almost $18,000 at auction.

 2000

AFLAC DUCK

WHY IT WORKS: Instead of quacking, this little white duck quips "Aflac"—the name of an insurance company. Although unusual, the ads are effective: The darling duck has helped make Aflac one of the most well-known companies in the world.

 2014 😊

PLATY THE PLATYPUS / JACKIE THE JACKALOPE

WHY IT WORKS: Symbolizing the "mixed-up fun" offered in Lunchables® meals, these animal mashups (one real, one mythical) make kids LOL with their quirky commercials and silly humor.

😊 1965 😊

POPPIN' FRESH (PILLSBURY DOUGHBOY)

WHY IT WORKS: This blue-eyed doughboy warmed hearts everywhere after people first saw him spring out from a can of Pillsbury crescent rolls. And it's still hard to resist the sound of his signature giggle after he's poked in his doughy belly. Poppin' Fresh has starred in more than 600 commercials and has had his own float in the Macy's Thanksgiving Day Parade.

UP CUTE and Personal

On their own, a monkey, a puppy, and a baby are arguably some of the most endearing things on Earth. But blend them together in an odd, dancing CGI mascot, and the result is more creepy than cute. That's what happened with a spot for Mountain Dew soda, where the "PuppyMonkeyBaby" wiggled its way onto TV screens during the 2016 Super Bowl. Ultimately, the ad didn't have the intended effect and raised more eyebrows than cheers.

Cute FASHION

ADORABLE is always on trend! From darling dresses to sneakers decorated with stuffed animals, here's a roundup of the snuggliest styles around, from top to bottom.

ALL DOLLED UP

For a fashion show in São Paulo, Brazil, designers drew inspiration from manga characters, the superpopular characters featured in Japanese comic books. Other major fashion houses, including Chanel, have offered a nod to manga culture by sending models with busy and brightly colored clothes and pastel-hued hair down the runway.

BEAR IT

No need to bring your favorite stuffed bear from place to place when you can simply slip on these shoes. The fuzzy sneakers—which feature teddy bear heads and spread-out arms around the tongue—ensure that you look cute from head to toe.

HERE, KITTY, KITTY

At the Cat Festival in Ypres, Belgium, kitties—like this fashionable feline—rule! Held every three years on the second Sunday in May, the celebration includes costumes, a parade, and plenty of parties to commemorate a medieval tradition in which cats were thrown from a tower to ward off witches. Thankfully, only toy cats are tossed into the crowd these days.

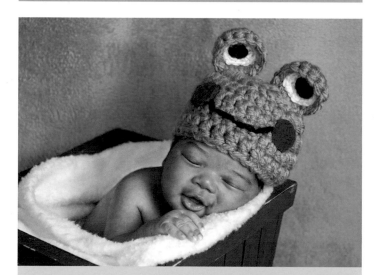

HATS OFF

What's cuter than a brand-new baby? How about one wearing a frog hat! This too-cute topper, crocheted to look like an adorable amphibian, is the perfect accessory for this slumbering infant. Sweet dreams!

MADE IN THE SHADES

What's a dog to do on a sunny day? Pop on some fruity—and fashionable!—shades, of course. While this pooch's pair are just for show, some companies sell dog-friendly sun goggles to protect your pet's peepers from harmful UV rays.

Style **CITY**

In Harajuku, a Tokyo neighborhood known for its out-there style, every day is like Halloween. Stroll the streets and you're sure to see residents roaming along dressed in the brightest, boldest, and most adorable outfits. The trend sparked in the 1980s as part of the Kawaii craze, when local teenagers mixed traditional Japanese attire with Western looks—like a multicolored kimono paired with platform sneakers. Today, just about anything goes, and the funkier, the better. From stuffed animal accessories to all-rainbow everything, Harajuku brings out the kid in everyone.

A CAREER IN Cute!

WHO: Judy Avey-Arroyo
WHAT: Founder of the Sloth Sanctuary of Costa Rica
WHERE: Limón Province, Costa Rica

JUDY AVEY-ARROYO has dedicated her life to working with some of the cutest things on Earth: sloths! As the founder of the Sloth Sanctuary of Costa Rica, Judy channeled her passion for animals into action and now leads efforts to protect and care for sloths rescued around her country. Here, Judy shares how a chance encounter with a baby sloth sparked a lifelong respect for the animals—and led to what some people call a dream job.

"People in Costa Rica used to think of sloths as pests—even wildlife facilities and zoos didn't know how to care for them. One day in 1992, three neighbor girls found an orphaned infant sloth. The girls knew we loved animals, so they brought it to us. We did not know what a baby sloth needed, so we watched the wild sloths on our property, then fed the baby fresh tree leaves and warmed goat's milk (a digestible substitute for sloth mother's milk). We named her Buttercup and were thrilled to see her gain the necessary weight and strength to survive. After that, people began bringing us injured and orphaned sloths, and I realized it was my calling to care for these beautiful and unusual animals.

"Five years after Buttercup came into our lives, my husband and I had our property officially recognized as a sloth rescue center. It was important for us to educate Costa Ricans about sloths. Today, my family and I enjoy sharing everything we know with people from around the world and right here in Costa Rica, too.

"My favorite part of what I do is helping people understand these animals. Sloths are so unusual: They have complex digestive tracts like cows and body temperatures like reptiles. I really enjoy seeing kids learning about sloths and why they are unique creatures.

"Sloth mothers frequently need to abandon their babies if they sense the baby is too weak to survive. We rescue the infant, bottle-feed it, and keep it warm in an incubator. Most of the babies gain weight and strength and eventually grow to be healthy adults, and it's the best feeling when we see a baby sloth survive and thrive.

"We treat injured adult sloths in our 'Slothpital' and set up a plan for them to recover and return to the forest. I've seen them look directly into my eyes as if to say, 'I was in pain, but I'm feeling better now, and I'm hungry for some delicious leaves!' It's like they know we are helping them.

"Nothing is cuter than a baby sloth's yawn! Its small mouth slowly opens, a tiny tongue sticks out, then *yawwwwn!*

"Sloths may be cute, but they are not pets. People dream of having a sloth as if it were a cat or dog, but that is unhealthy for the sloth. We encourage sloth lovers to respect them from a distance and not need to touch or hold them. Even the cutest wild animals need to be appreciated from afar.

"I love what I do, but in a perfect world, we would not need a sloth sanctuary. Humans invading rain forest habitats is causing an unbalanced environment for these animals. They are losing their home. We hope our work here will inspire kids and give them the power to influence others to work together to save Earth's rain forests and all of the animals that live there."

Ziggy was orphaned and rescued from a nearby village. He arrived very hungry and thirsty, and was covered with a fungus rash. With veterinary treatment, Ziggy's skin healed well, and he has been gaining the necessary weight that is so important for infant sloths to grow into strong, healthy adults.

Before releasing Stacy, an adult *Choloepus*, back to the rain forest, Judy examines her closely. Stacy has an ID bracelet and sometimes passes back through the sanctuary trees as she forages for leaves.

HONEY, I shrunk the laptop! How some people and companies are downsizing their products for bigger business.

mini

MAKEOVERS!

DRONES

THIS: Regular drone
TO THAT: Mini drone
This tiny gadget—no bigger than a Matchbox car—can fly in any direction and snaps still photos and videos. And because it's so small, you don't need a license to fly it, which is required in many places for standard-size personal drones.

LAPTOP COMPUTERS

THIS: Regular laptop
TO THAT: Mini laptop
With a seven-inch (18-cm) screen, this computer—said to be the world's smallest—is more suitable to be perched in your palm than on your lap.

TABLETS

THIS: iPad (standard size)
TO THAT: iPad mini
Same technology, smaller size. Apple's trimmed-down tablet also comes with a reduced price, making it popular among parents buying it for their kids.

VIDEO GAMES

THIS: Original Nintendo console
TO THAT: NES Classic Edition
When Nintendo first released this shrunken throwback of its classic '80s console in 2016, it sold out almost right away. Nintendo rereleased the NES Classic Edition back into stores in 2018, and it proved to still be popular, with pre-sales soaring months before it even hit the stores.

CAMERAS

THIS: Standard-size camera
TO THAT: Mini camera
About as wide as a quarter, this camera is tiny enough to rest on your finger. Despite its dainty size, the camera takes high-res images and even shoots video!

CLEAN SWEEP

Well, hello there! Even rather boring tasks like vacuuming can be fun when pushing around Henry, this friendly-faced appliance.

ADORABLE Appliances

A cute toaster? An adorable oven?

YEP, THAT'S RIGHT! The darling designs of these appliances tap into our natural love of all things precious. Here's how some businesses have harnessed the power of cute to sell appealing alternatives to standard household items.

IT'S A WASH

Doing dishes doesn't feel like such a chore when loading them into this retro-style dishwasher, available in a rainbow of pastel colors, like turquoise and beach blue.

SO COOL

Made by Italian company Smeg, these fun fridges come in a variety of bright colors. A colorful fridge may be cute, but it'll cost you: These fridges run up to $3,000.

TO A TEA

You'll want to whistle for this charming kettle, featuring an adorable giraffe. The giraffe's neck doubles as the kettle's handle!

POP-UP

It's a Hello Kitty world, we're just living in it. Case in point: this too-cute toaster, which browns an image of the famous icon on every slice it toasts.

DUCK FACE

This smart speaker is just ducky! The portable bluetooth-enabled gadget can tell you the weather, share a joke, or play your favorite tunes with a quick voice command.

HELLO KITTY

The world's **biggest rubber duck** is as tall as a six-story building.

HI-TECH Cute

Who says robots can't be lovable? Sure, they're created in a factory, are full of wires, and need to be charged every few hours, but some of today's high-tech bots are all about making you smile. Here's how some companies are capitalizing on their customers' love of cute to create technology that truly livens things up.

HELLO, MY PET

Allergic to dogs? That doesn't mean you'll never be able to have a pet pooch. Thanks to robots like Sony's Aibo, you can have a constant companion built just for you. This four-legged, $1,700 bot (currently available only in Japan) relies on sensors and built-in cameras to respond to your commands and voice. It plays fetch, wags its tail when you pet it, rolls over, and even looks at you with various versions of puppy dog eyes. In fact, Aibo does almost everything an actual dog does—except for shed and drool.

If a cat is more your bag, you can scoop up a robo-kitty that's made to look and act like the real deal. A team of scientists is currently working to add artificial intelligence to a robotic cat, mostly focusing on providing company to the elderly. The bot has soft fur, purrs, meows, rolls over to request a belly rub—and will be programmed to remind its human to take medicine or go to an appointment. Now that's a clever cat.

YOU'VE GOT A FRIEND

You know those days when you just need a friend to listen to you? Well, there's a bot for that. Experts are developing robotic companions that show compassion to humans. Bots like Buddy by Blue Frog Robotics use sensors, cameras, facial recognition, and microphones to hear and speak, plus they can show off a range of expressions from smiles to sadness. Companion bots are also programmed to play games, let you video chat with a friend, and can even warn you if something's wrong at your house. Sounds like these pals are the complete package.

This **BB-8™ by Sphero**—a replica of the Star Wars droid—recognizes and reacts to your voice.

ROBOTIC DOG

ROBOTIC CAT

BB-8™ by Sphero

BUDDY

CHAPTER 6

EVERYDAY
Adorable

IT'S HARD to escape cute. A lot of what goes on in your life—from what you wear to what you click on—has to do with its inviting appeal. Think about it: Nearly every single day, we share *aww*-inducing images with our friends, cuddle with our favorite pets, and watch hilarious animated (and adorable) characters on TV. Sometimes, lovable things can lift your spirits and help you get healthier—or maybe one day, they'll become a part of your career. Want to learn more about how cute plays different roles in our day-to-day lives? Read on.

Cute TO THE RESCUE

THERE'S NO QUESTION that being around anything cute and cuddly can make you happier. But sometimes, the power of cute can extend beyond just making you smile. Here are six ways that interaction with the snuggly and sweet can lift people's spirits—and change lives for the better.

DO-GOODER DOG

Norbert, a registered therapy dog, spreads smiles to children sick in the hospital. The tiny mixed breed—he weighs just 3.5 pounds (1.6 kg)—has been featured in two books and even has a stuffed animal modeled after him.

TEACHER'S PET

Across the country, **puppies** are popping up in classrooms as part of their training to become guide dogs for the blind. Not only does the exposure to young kids help the dogs learn to be calm and well mannered, the students benefit, too: Studies show that having an animal in the classroom may help kids stay on task and become more excited about learning.

STUDY BUDDIES

Thanks to programs that bring puppies to college campuses, students across the country get a much welcome study break by cuddling up to **four-legged friends.** Because college may be tough, but even the most stressed-out student can't help but giggle after being licked by a puppy!

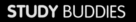

HOP TO IT

Blossom is so much more than your basic stuffed bunny. Equipped with technology that allows it to react to content in videos, this still-in-development soft robot may one day be used as a companion and teaching tool for kids on the autism spectrum.

COMING OUT OF HER **SHELL**

Try not to smile when you see a **63-pound** (29-kg) **tortoise** moseying around in a dress! Meet therapy tortoise Wasabi (named because she's "hot stuff," naturally). This African spurred tortoise visits hospitals and schools to spread cheer and fill hearts with joy just by being a calm—and cute—presence around people in need.

WHAT A **DOLL**

Lifelike dolls are used in nursing homes to soothe and provide company to elderly residents. Some experts say that holding and tending to a doll can reduce anxiety and bring comfort to those suffering from dementia and Alzheimer's disease.

Hey, **BABY**

Images of babies can soften the hearts of just about anyone—and they may even fight crime! At least that's what one town in the United Kingdom is going for in having local artists paint images of infants on a shop's shutters. The theory behind the paintings is that these super-sweet images may have a calming effect on would-be robbers and vandals, which may lead them to have a change of heart before they do anything criminal. Plus, the happy images portray the area as safe and friendly.

(Tiny)
HELPiNG

VICTORIA NODIFF-NETANEL and her volunteers load her crew of mini therapy horses into the back of her van and hit the road. Soon, Pearl, Willow Blue, Liberty Bell, American Valor, Blue Moon, Sweet Louise, and Stormy Blue will be strolling the halls of the Ronald McDonald Houses in Los Angeles and Pasadena, California, U.S.A. The horses will stop to see patients, letting kids stroke their soft manes, wrap them in big hugs, or lead them down the hallway on leashes. Sometimes, they'll show off with tricks like standing on hind legs to a "Hi-Ho Silver!" command, playing a keyboard, or "smiling" when prompted.

MINI AND MAGICAL

Studies show that being around a cute and cuddly animal can boost your spirits. And for those who are sick or going through tough times, animals can offer a powerful form of therapy. As Victoria's mini horses demonstrate, even tiny therapy animals can make a huge impression. The California-based nonprofit organization Mini Therapy Horses is so popular that Victoria makes weekly visits to adult hospitals, as well as those for children. They've even been featured in the Rose Parade. They also visit families who have recently lost a loved one, and Victoria brings them to college campuses to de-stress students before final exams.

"They have this calming effect, and they are just so cute," says Victoria of her pint-size pets, which are bred to be the size of a large dog. "They're like magical unicorns—people can't believe they are real."

TINY HORSES, BIG IMPRESSIONS

Mini horses are so appealing, says Victoria, because their size makes them accessible and intriguing. "Even if a child doesn't speak English, he can connect with a mini horse. All you have to do is spin your finger in a circle and they will twirl around," says Victoria. "The horses are so loving. It doesn't matter how old people are—everyone wants to pet them, touch them, and hug them. They may be little, but they have such a huge presence."

HOOVES

How mini horses provide "cute" therapy for kids in need.

CLICK ON THIS! There's a reason these photos have been shared around the world. They're just so darn adorable! Here's a roundup of the cutest, most shared, and most liked images out there.

CUTE GOES Viral!

FULL TILT

This precious pooch sets tongues wagging (2.1 million on Instagram, to be exact) with her oh-so-adorable images. A rescue pup, **Marnie the shih tzu** went from the streets to internet sensation, thanks to her endearing head tilt (likely the result of an earlier illness), big eyes, and extra-long tongue.

LOVE TAP

This underwater shot made a big splash when a sweet **hippo baby** born at a zoo in Berlin, Germany, was first introduced to the public. The nose-y nudge from Mom shows that even giant animals like hippos have a soft side.

GREAT ESCAPE

Rusty the **red panda** captivated the nation after a daring escape from the National Zoo in Washington, D.C. First exiting his exhibit through the tree canopy, Rusty then took a jaunt through a nearby neighborhood, where he was spotted by a passerby, who Tweeted out his picture. Hours later, Rusty was found and returned to the zoo—where he remains, safe and sound.

#SLOTHLOVE

A gallery of OMG images featuring snuggly (and sleepy) **baby sloths** at a rehab center was a megahit—and became some of the most shared images among those posted by National Geographic in 2016.

WHY SO GLUM?

You can't help but grin at this frowning kitty. Born with an underbite that gives her a perma-pout, **Tardar Sauce** aka Grumpy Cat became one of the most famous felines on Earth after a picture and video of her went viral in 2012. Today, Grumpy Cat is a magazine cover model, has appeared on Broadway, and has her own clothing line. Now that's something to smile about.

Sharing the
LOVE

What, exactly, makes certain videos and pictures so popular? Experts say there's a science behind images and videos that go viral. According to a study published in the journal *Computers in Human Behavior*, looking at pictures of precious things can make you less anxious, more energetic, and a little happier than before you saw the pics. Plus, because our brain processes images up to 60,000 times faster than words, those sweet shots of baby sloths or precious pups can make a quick impact on our mind. Finally, these pics are fun—and easy—to share: By sharing a quick post, people can bring smiles to hundreds of their friends' faces in a matter of milliseconds.

SAY CHEESE

The **quokkas'** selfie game is strong! Folks in Australia are clamoring to capture a shot with these friendly cat-size marsupials, mostly found on Rottnest Island near Perth. Some 23,000 people have posted pics on social media tagging it with—what else?—#quokkaselfie.

All Dressed Up

WHY IT'S CUTE:
Photographer Sioin Queenie Liao sure knows how to make the most of naptime! While her baby son Wengenn slept, she dressed him up in costumes and snapped away. The adorable images—featuring looks from a sushi chef to a mariner—racked up millions of likes online.

Adorable
ART

PETITE PAINTINGS, SLEEPING BABIES, and even precious portraits of rats (yes, rats!). Here are five ways artists have blended cute and creative.

Painting

WHY IT'S CUTE: Artist Brooke Rothshank's drawings may be small enough to fit on your thumbnail, but their wow factor is huge. To create her incredibly detailed and lifelike images, Rothshank uses watercolors and a superfine brush. But drawing them is no piece of, uh, pie: It can take her an entire day to complete just one painting.

By Design

WHY IT'S CUTE: Watch your art leap off the page and come to life through Budsies, which transforms a one-dimensional drawing into a detailed stuffed animal. How does it work? Simply snap a digital picture of your drawing, have a guardian help you send it to Budsies.com, and a team of designers and seamstresses will work to create a matching toy. Within seven weeks, you'll have a finished plush that's truly your own design.

Snack Time

WHY IT'S CUTE: Who says rats can't be cute? This trio of baby rats were meant to be snacks for snakes before they were rescued and raised by the photographer who snapped this perfectly timed shot of them munching on a cookie together.

For the Dogs

WHY IT'S CUTE: This art show is for the dogs—literally! "The Barking Project," a public art display in New York City, features sculptures and installations made specifically for dogs, like a pooch-shaped silhouette featuring a motion sensor that starts barking when anyone approaches. Bow *wow*.

Cutest JOBS EVER

YOU CALL THIS WORK?
These playful—and paid!—positions are almost too good to be true.

THE PERKS: Coming up with the ideas for custom—and clever—ducks, like "Harry Ponder," "Spa Wars," and "Duck the Magic Dragon."

"People love **rubber ducks.** There is something about the shape, the color, the feel, that is totally cute no matter how **young or old** you are."

—Craig Wolfe, president of CelebriDucks

HEDGEHOG **OFFICER**

THE PERKS: Working with developers, urban planners, and citizens to build a network of hedgehog-friendly routes, such as linking gardens in neighborhoods. (And yes, occasionally cuddling with the spiky critters, too.)

"There is still **so much to learn** about these night-time visitors and this piques my natural curiosity, but one thing I do hear a lot is how people are **seeing less** of them. So I want to do whatever I can to help the plight of this popular British species."

— Emily Wilson, hedgehog officer for Hedgehog Street, a campaign intent on increasing the animal's dwindling numbers in the U.K.

CAT **CUDDLER**

THE PERKS: Curl up with a kitty and pet its soft fur—and get paid while you're at it! This full-time job is focused on keeping cats calm when they visit the vet.

"The ideal candidate must have **gentle hands** capable of petting cats for long periods of time. They need to be capable of cat whispering to **calm the nerves** of some of our inpatients. An ability to **understand** different types of purring is a distinct added advantage."

—Job listing at Just Cats Veterinary Clinic in Dublin, Ireland

Some pet haircuts take two or more hours to complete.

PROFESSIONAL PET STYLIST

THE PERKS: Work with cats, dogs, and the occasional guinea pig to fluff up their fur, trim their toenails, and give them a makeover that they'll meow ... or bark ... over. Bonus points if pets wind up looking like a stuffed animal.

"These cuts truly are **works of art.** The emphasis ... is to make the [pet] look as adorable as possible by highlighting [its] **uniquely cute** characteristics."

— Photographer Grace Chon, who documented done-up dogs for a photo series called "Hairy"

PANDA **NANNY**

THE PERKS: Hanging out with, cuddling, feeding, and cleaning up after panda cubs—all while increasing awareness of the beloved bears.

"Your work has only **one mission:** spending **365 days** with the pandas and sharing in their joys and sorrows."

—Organizers at the Giant Panda Protection and Research Center in China's Sichuan Province, which works to increase numbers of pandas in the wild through conservation programs

VOICE-OVER **ACTOR**

THE PERKS: A cute and quirky voice can help you land starring roles in animated TV series, video games, and commercials, and even be immortalized in talking toys.

"I was called **'squeaky'** since grade school. One day, my teacher told me that nobody was going to **take me seriously** in the real world unless I did something about my voice. So I did."

—Lisa Biggs, a voice-over actor in Charlotte, North Carolina, U.S.A., and the voice behind the talking StarLily My Magical Unicorn and the animated show Badanamu Cadets

CHAPTER 7

ADORABLE
IN Action

SNUGGLY SPORTING EVENTS that make you squeal with delight. Snaps of adorably energetic pets and people caught in action. Charming cars that will, well, move you ... and make you melt. Yes, cute things are definitely here, there, and everywhere! From precious planes to puppies playing sports, here's a broader look into all of the cute things that go.

CAUGHT BEING
Cute!

These awesome action shots create the most adorable moments frozen in time.

SNUGGLE BUDDIES

How *otterly* adorable! These sea otters snuggle up as they float in an aquarium exhibit. In both captivity and the wild, sea otters often hold hands while they sleep and eat so that family members don't drift away from each other.

ROLL ON

Skateboarding dogs are totally a thing—and they're totally cute. One brave bulldog named Otto (not pictured) set a world record by skating through a human tunnel of 30 legs at an event in Peru.

MONKEYING AROUND

Yee-haw! Whiplash the cowboy capuchin monkey makes people smile around the world by ripping around rodeo rings and rounding up sheep on the back of a border collie. The rescue monkey has also made halftime appearances at professional football games.

TINY BUBBLES

Many photographers rely on good timing—and a lot of luck—to capture one-of-a-kind images. Babies can't stay underwater for long, so this precious photo had to be snapped in seconds.

93

DIAPER Dash

WHY IT'S CUTE: The fact that they can't walk yet doesn't slow these babies down. The littlest athletes **test their crawling speed** by dashing down a mini racetrack.

WINNING FACT: One recent Diaper Dash champ won **free diapers for a year**—and all of the baby bragging rights.

CUTEST
Competition

FROM THE START to the finish line, these adorable athletic events are truly winners.

BUNNY
High Jump

WHY IT'S CUTE: These rabbits may not have wings, but they can sure soar! In Kaninhop events, cuddly bunnies **test their jumping skills** by zooming over barriers and leaping great lengths. It's truly a hopping-good time.

WINNING FACT: A rabbit once cleared a **height of 39.2 inches** (99.5 cm) in this competition.

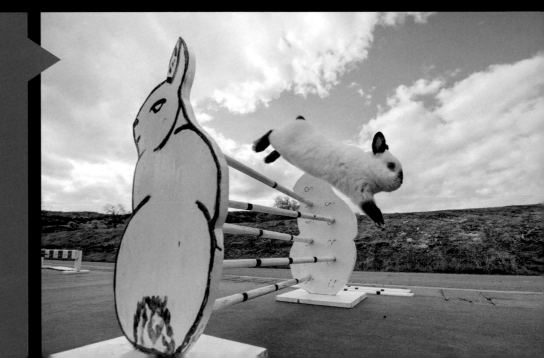

PUPPY Bowl

WHY IT'S CUTE: Furry foes take to a mini football field and go paw-to-paw in a televised game that's truly for the dogs. And the teams' mascots— **a chinchilla and a screech owl**—are equally adorable.

WINNING FACT: Each of the puppy players—which range in ages from **12 to 20 weeks**—are available for adoption.

Sue Ryder MASCOT Gold Cup

WHY IT'S CUTE: More than 100 mascots—from **big-headed bears to bumblebees**—attempt to outsprint each other in this 200-m (656-foot) grassy dash to raise money for hospice care.

WINNING FACT: The 2015 event set a **world record** for the largest mascot race, with 125 participants.

STARLIGHT Run

WHY IT'S CUTE: At this 5K (3.1-mile) road race in Portland, Oregon, U.S.A., those dressed up in clever costumes are the real winners. Each year offers a different dress-up theme—and mega-awards for the cutest looks. Past participants have shown up as everything from these **summer swimmers to a big block of cheese.**

WINNING FACT: More than **250,000 spectators** line the streets to cheer for the costumed competitors.

Adorable WAYS
TO GET AROUND

CHARMING CARS, precious planes, and to-die-for trains:
These vehicles are some of the cutest ways
to get from here to there.

SHRUNKEN SPORTS CAR

Talk about a compact car! This little electric **Lamborghini**—built by a Chinese farmer for his grandson—can drive as far as 60 miles (97 km) when fully charged.

ALL ABOARD

This train features the likeness of Tama, a female **calico cat** who gained fame for being a station master and operating officer at Kishi—Tama(Cat)—Station on the Kishigawa Line in Kinokawa, Wakayama, Japan.

FLYING KITTY

No doubt, **Hello Kitty** is everywhere—even at 36,000 feet (11,000 m) above the Earth! With one Asia-based airline's Hello Kitty–themed airplanes, passengers get treated to HK everything. In addition to the plane's exterior, its seats, pillows, utensils, wet wipes, and even air-sickness bags are all decorated with the cuddly cartoon character's face.

FOR THE DOGS

Luigi Maestro is one pampered pooch. The shih tzu has a collection of **luxury cars**—including a BMW and a Bentley—to roll around the streets of New York City in. The dog-size remote-controlled car collection costs around $1,500.

BUG LOVE

The classic Volkswagen Beetle—which first hit U.S. roads in 1949—has been updated through the years to appear more friendly. People even add **eyelashes** to the headlights to complete the lovable look.

Driven to CUTE?

When it comes to which cars many consumers are drawn to, experts say it's all about that face. It's no surprise that many cars look like faces from the front, and one study shows that looking at a car can trigger the same area of our brain that's activated for human facial recognition. While softening a vehicle's "face" (think: big headlights for eyes and a round body) may boost its cute factor, the same can't be said for the actual sales of cars. Research says that people are more interested in buying cars that appear more intimidating and powerful on the roads, which means they opt for models with a more "angry" mug.

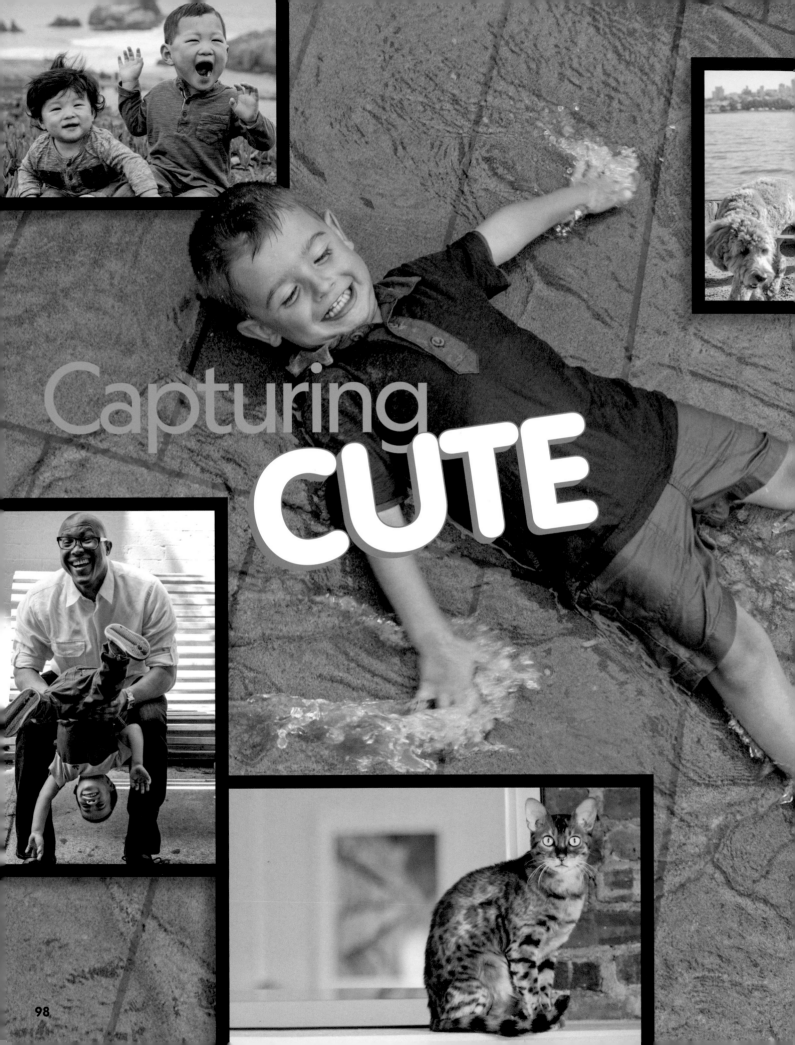

Capturing CUTE

WHO: Sarah Sloboda
WHAT: Family and pet photographer
WHERE: San Francisco, California, U.S.A.

Q: What do you love most about photographing babies, kids, and pets?

A: Babies and kids have a strong connection to their inner world. They have gentle energy. They know how to talk to animals and feel the breeze in the air that is full of magic and possibility. Their energy is fun and soothing to be around.

Q: How do you get your subjects to be comfortable in front of the camera?

A: A camera can make anyone a little bit scared and nervous. So I joke around with them and try to play games. I say something silly that gets people to think about fun things.

Q: Any tips or tricks for getting kids to act natural?

A: A lot of kids have had their picture taken thousands of times because everyone around has a smartphone. Parents will ask kids to "hold still," "smile," and "say cheese." The faces kids make when they hold still and smile are not the same as when they are having fun and laughing. I have kids run and laugh and dance. Or I'll ask them to think nice thoughts and look right at the camera. The camera will pick up those emotions.

Q: What about pets? How do you get a dog or cat to sit still and make eye contact with the camera?

A: Animals are very interested in a lot of other things and can get easily distracted. Sometimes with dogs, I will hold a treat or a toy in my hand near the camera and call their name. But mostly, it is important to be patient and to have my finger ready to press the shutter very fast. Because often when an animal looks at the camera, it is only for a split second.

Q: What tips or advice do you have for kids who want to get into photography?

A: If you have access to a camera of any kind, start taking pictures of your favorite things. When I was a kid, I used to pose my dolls and build things out of Lincoln Logs and take pictures of them. Use the camera to focus on the specific things you would like to document about your life— create a story with pictures. Take pictures at all different angles and experiment with different types of light like lamps, windows, the sun, a big white wall. And have fun! Remember, a great photograph doesn't have to look exactly like life. It's all about how you capture the magic and energy of that very moment.

Drawing "CUTE"

MEET THE ARTIST:

AS A PROFESSIONAL ILLUSTRATOR, Dona Teare makes a living drawing things. Her whimsical illustrations have appeared in children's books and public murals in places like her hometown of Rockville, Maryland, U.S.A. Here, Dona details how she got her start and what she loves about being an artist, and she also shares some simple steps on drawing your own *aww*-some illustrations!

"Ever since I was little, I've loved to draw. Growing up, I always had colored pencils and a sketchbook with me. I'd draw mostly dogs, cats, and other animals.

"I had a talent for drawing from the start, but I also worked hard on it. Like any skill, art takes time and practice. I drew all the time, and I'd look to other artists for inspiration. When I wasn't drawing, I'd be at the library looking up books by my favorite artists, like Frida Kahlo.

"My style is definitely cute and cartoony. I still love to draw animals, and I'm a fan of drawing fruit, too. I usually put eyes on everything. I think adding big, wide eyes to simple things makes them really come alive.

"I sometimes illustrate on the computer, but I still like to get my hands dirty. I prefer to paint or sketch on paper.

"My advice for anyone out there who loves to draw is to keep practicing! Don't be afraid to stick to your own style if you're happy with it. Remember, drawing is meant to be fun and creative."

Ready to draw your own adorable animals? Here's how!

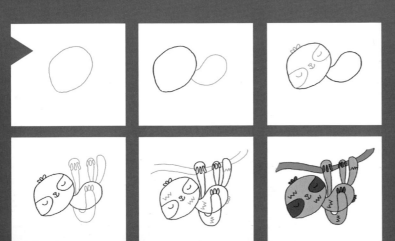

Sloth

1. Draw a slightly tilted oval.
2. Add a bean shape.
3. Draw in the face and hair bumps, keeping the eyes and mouth almost at the same level on the face.
4. Add four limbs and some claws.
5. Draw in a branch and furry details.
6. Color and smile at the sloth's cuteness!

Panda

1. Draw an oval.
2. Add a bean-shaped body.
3. Draw circles for the ears, eyes, nose and mouth.
4. Add arms, legs and a tail.
5. Add in a detail, like a belly and a leaf sprig.
6. Color and admire your drawing!

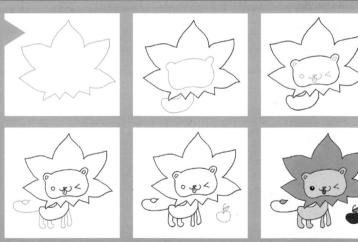

Monkey

1. Draw a rounded square.
2. Add a bean-shaped body.
3. Draw in the facial features and ears, keeping the eyes far apart and the nose on the same level as the eyes. The mouth is a rounded triangle.
4. Add four limbs and an extra-long tail.
5. Add in a detail, like a bunch of bananas.
6. Color and adore!

Lion

1. Draw a leaf shape that's slightly squished at the bottom.
2. Inside the leaf shape, draw a bean shape with nubs. Draw another bean shape for the body outside of the leaf.
3. Draw in the face—make one eye winking if you want!
4. Draw in legs and a tail.
5. Add a detail like an apple.
6. Color and enjoy your lion!

Tiger

1. Draw a lima bean shape.
2. Add a smaller bean shape.
3. Draw the face and ears, keeping the eyes and nose on the same level and the eyes far apart.
4. Add four limbs and an extra-long tail.
5. Add in stripes and a detail, like an umbrella.
6. Color and you're finished!

Test Your CUTE IQ!

THINK YOU KNOW it all about all things adorable? Take this quiz to test your smarts! (Stumped? Flip back through the previous pages ... All of the answers are in this book and also appear at the bottom of page 103.)

1. According to researcher Konrad Lorenz, what characteristic makes a baby so cute?
   A. A large, round head
   B. Chubby cheeks
   C. Big eyes
   D. All of the above

2. True or False: Some spiders have hairy feet that look like mini dog paws.

3. What is "Kawaii"?
   A. The Japanese term used for anything adorable
   B. The Japanese term used for any type of animal
   C. A Hawaiian island
   D. The 1992 Olympic mascot

4. Which famous catchphrase did Charlie® the Tuna popularize in StarKist® tuna commercials?
   A. "Better luck next time!"
   B. "Sorry, Charlie!"
   C. "See you later, alligator!"
   D. "D'oh!"

5. True or False: The smell of babies may trigger intense happiness.

6. Hello Kitty, a multibillion-dollar brand, launched which of the following?
   A. A line of airplanes
   B. A line of toasters
   C. A café
   D. All of the above

7. True or False: A veterinary clinic in Ireland once hired a turtle cuddler to keep the reptiles calm during visits.

8. Fill in the blank. A cucamelon is a fruit that looks like a watermelon, tastes like cucumber and lime, and is the size of a _____.

9. The tiny bee fly served as the inspiration for which Pokémon character?
   A. Squirtle
   B. Beedrill
   C. Cutiefly
   D. Butterfree

10. Fill in the blank. A panda's black eye patches make its eyes appear _____ times bigger than they actually are.

Index

Index

Index

Credits

Sanrio; 59 (UP RT), Daniel Banks; 59 (LO RT), Aflo/REX/Shutterstock; 60 (UP RT), Mari Taoka; 60 (LO RT), Tammi Colleary-Loach; 60 (LO CTR), Taiyaki, NYC; 60 (CTR LE), photo by Dominique Ansel Bakery; 61 (UP LE), Laurel Wassner; 61 (UP RT), WichitS/Getty Images; 61 (LO RT), Olgaorly/Getty Images; 61 (LO LE), Sann von Mai/Shutterstock; **Chapter 5:** 62-63, TY Lim/Shutterstock; 64 (Michelin), Courtesy Michelin; 64 (Morton), ®The Umbrella Girl design mark is a registered trademark of Morton Salt, Inc.; 64 (Coppertone), The Advertising Archives/Alamy Stock Photo; 64 (Pillsbury), Use with permission of General Mills; 64 (Charlie), Courtesy StarKist®; 65 (Energizer), The Energizer Bunny design and Still Going are trademarks of Energizer Brands, LLC and are used with permission; 65 (Aflac), Courtesy Aflac; 65 (Platy-Jackie), The Platy the Platypus and Jackie the Jackelope images and LUNCHABLES trademark is owned by Kraft Heinz Foods Company and is used with permission; 65 (Snuggle), Reproduced with kind permission of Unilever PLC and group companies/Reproduced with permission from Henkel Corporation; 66 (UP), Sebastiao Moreira/EPA/REX/Shutterstock; 66 (LO), andersphoto/Shutterstock; 67 (UP), Natalka-Prague/Getty Images; 67 (CTR RT), Fernando Trabanco Fotografia/Getty Images; 67 (LO LE), Katrina Trninich/Dreamstime; 69 (ALL), Ray Richardson; 70-71, Richard Newstead/Getty Images; 70 (CTR), Courtesy Aukey; 70 (LO RT), Courtesy GPD; 71 (ipads), Denys Prykhodov/Shutterstock; 71 (full NES), Neil Godwin/Future/REX/Shutterstock; 71 (mini NES), Guillaume Payen/SOPA Images/LightRocket via Getty Images; 71 (camera), indiaforte/Alamy Stock Photo; 71 (mini camera),

Hammacher Schlemmer/Solent News/Rex/Shutterstock; 72 (UP LE), Alisdair Macdonald/REX/Shutterstock; 72 (CTR LE), Courtesy Big Chill; 72 (LO), Richard B. Levine/Newscom; 73 (UP LE), KitchenRus/Supreme Housewares; 73 (UP RT), Yoshikazu Tsuno/AFP/Getty Images; 73 (LO), Courtesy Clova; 74 (CTR), Aflo/REX/Shutterstock; 74 (LO), Stephan Savoia/AP/REX/Shutterstock; 75, Eric Piermont/AFP/Getty Images; 75 (UP LE), bryan rowe; **Chapter 6:** 76-77, aldomurillo/Getty Images; 78 (UP RT), Gabriel Olsen/Getty Images; 78 (LO RT), Liliya Kulianionak/Shutterstock; 78 (LO LE), Courtesy Sarah Wassner Flynn; 79 (UP LE), Michael Suguitan/Cornell University; 79 (UP RT), Lisa Chicarella; 79 (LO LE), Santiago Urquijo/Getty Images; 80 (LO), Courtesy Mini Therapy Horses; 81 (UP), Courtesy Mini Therapy Horses; 82 (CTR LE), Z5327 Soeren Stache Deutsch Presse Agentur/Newscom; 82 (CTR), Benjamin Lozovsky/BFA/REX/Shutterstock; 82 (LO RT), Getty Images News/Getty Images; 83 (UP), Sam Trull; 83 (CTR), Nils Jorgensen/REX/Shutterstock; 83 (LO), see-shooteatrepeat/Shutterstock; 84 (UP), Sioin Queenie Liao/Wengenn In Wonderland; 84 (LO), Brooke Rothshank; 85 (UP), Courtesy Budsies; 85 (CTR LE), Diane Özdamar Photography & Illustration; 85 (LO RT), AP/REX/Shutterstock; 86, Courtesy Celebriducks; 87 (UP), Carmelka/Getty Images; 87 (CTR), Jaap Arriens/NurPhoto via Getty Images; 88, Africa Studio/Shutterstock; 89 (UP), VCG/VCG via Getty Images; 89 (LO LE), Courtesy Lisa Biggs; 89 (Starlily), The furReal STARLILY, MY MAGICAL UNICORN name and images are property of Hasbro, Inc. used with permission. © 2018 Hasbro, Inc.; 89 (Jess), Badanamu/Calm Island Inc; **Chapter 7:** 90-91, Ruaridh Connellan/

Barcroft Images/Barcroft Media via Getty Images; 92-93, Laurentiu Garofeanu/Barcroft USA/Barcroft Media via Getty Images; 93 (UP LE), Chelsea Lauren/WireImage/Getty Images; 93 (UP RT), Tom Soucek/National Geographic Creative; 93 (LO RT), Andrey Nekrasov/Barcroft Images/Barcroft Media via Getty Images; 93 (LO CTR), Dan Callister/REX/Shutterstock; 94 (UP), Dominick Reuter/AFP/Getty Images; 94 (LO), Waz Fotopool/Action Press; 95 (UP), Linda Davidson/The Washington Post via Getty Images; 95 (CTR), Alan Carmichael/Capricorn Photography; 95 (LO), Waz-Mix Pix/Courtesy Starlight Run; 96 (CTR), VCG/VCG via/Getty Images; 96 (LO), By Duke of arcH - www.flickr.com/photos/dukeofarch/Getty Images; 97 (UP), The Asahi Shimbun via Getty Images; 97 (CTR), Ruaridh Connellan/Barcroft-Images/Barcroft Media via Getty Images; 97 (LO), energyy/Getty Images; 98-99 (ALL), Sarah Sloboda Photography; **End Matter:** 100 (UP), opicobello/Shutterstock; 100 (LO), Dona Teare Illustrations; 101 (ALL), Dona Teare Illustrations; 102, STR/AFP/Getty Images; 103 (UP LE), Donhype/iStockPhoto/Getty Images; 103 (UP RT), John Carnemolla/iStockPhoto/Getty Images; 103 (LO RT), He Yujun/Dreamstime; 103 (LO LE), Estersinhache fotografia/Getty Images; 103 (CTR LE), Image Source/Getty Images

To the cutest wonders in my world: Eamon, Nora, and Nell
—SWF

Since 1888, the National Geographic Society has funded more than 12,000 research, exploration, and preservation projects around the world. The Society receives funds from National Geographic Partners, LLC, funded in part by your purchase. A portion of the proceeds from this book supports this vital work. To learn more, visit natgeo.com/info.

NATIONAL GEOGRAPHIC and Yellow Border Design are trademarks of the National Geographic Society, used under license.

For more information, visit nationalgeographic.com, call 1-800-647-5463, or write to the following address:

National Geographic Partners
1145 17th Street N.W.
Washington, D.C. 20036-4688 U.S.A.

Visit us online at nationalgeographic.com/books

For librarians and teachers: ngchildrensbooks.org

More for kids from National Geographic: natgeokids.com

National Geographic Kids magazine inspires children to explore their world with fun yet educational articles on animals, science, nature, and more. Using fresh storytelling and amazing photography, *Nat Geo Kids* shows kids ages 6 to 14 the fascinating truth about the world—and why they should care. kids.nationalgeographic.com/subscribe

For information about special discounts for bulk purchases, please contact National Geographic Books Special Sales: specialsales@natgeo.com

For rights or permissions inquiries, please contact National Geographic Books Subsidiary Rights: bookrights@natgeo.com

Designed by Jim Hiscott

The publisher would like to thank everyone who made this book possible: Ariane Szu-Tu, editor; Sarah J. Mock, senior photo editor; Kathryn Robbins, art director; Joan Gossett, production editor; Anne Leong-Son and Gus Tello, design production assistants.

Library of Congress Cataloging-in-Publication Data
Names: Flynn, Sarah Wassner, author. I National Geographic Kids (Firm),
    publisher. I National Geographic Society (U.S.)
Title: This book is cute / by Sarah Wassner Flynn.
Description: Washington, DC : National Geographic Kids, [2019] I Audience:
    Ages 8-12. I Audience: Grades 4 to 6. I Includes index.
Identifiers: LCCN 2018035953I ISBN 9781426332944 (pbk.) I ISBN 9781426332951 (hardcover)
Subjects: LCSH: Appearance (Philosophy)--Juvenile literature. I Physical-
    appearance-based bias--Juvenile literature. I Preferences (Philosophy)--
    Juvenile literature. I Aesthetics--Juvenile literature. I Neoteny--Juvenile literature.
Classification: LCC B105.A66 F59 2019 I DDC 152--dc23
    LC record available at https://lccn.loc.gov/2018035953

Printed in China
18/RRDS/1